Vaughan Williams for Choirs 2

JOHN LEAVITT

10 secular pieces compiled and arranged for
accompanied and unaccompanied mixed voices

MUSIC DEPARTMENT

OXFORD

UNIVERSITY PRESS

OXFORD
UNIVERSITY PRESS

Great Clarendon Street, Oxford OX2 6DP,
United Kingdom

Oxford University Press is a department of the University of Oxford.
It furthers the University's objective of excellence in research, scholarship,
and education by publishing worldwide. Oxford is a registered trade mark of
Oxford University Press in the UK and in certain other countries

First published 2020

Impression: 1

ISBN 978-0-19-353209-0

Music and text origination by Andrew Jones
Printed in Great Britain on acid-free paper by
Halstan & Co. Ltd, Amersham, Bucks.

Contents

Preface

Welcome to this collection of new arrangements of short choral pieces by one of the finest British composers of the twentieth century. Born in 1872 in Gloucestershire, Ralph Vaughan Williams attended the Royal College of Music and read history and music at Trinity College, Cambridge. He studied composition with C. Hubert H. Parry and Charles Villiers Stanford, and received further tuition overseas from Max Bruch and Maurice Ravel. After a distinguished career, producing a particularly wide-ranging catalogue of works, Vaughan Williams died on 26 August 1958. His ashes were interred at Westminster Abbey.

Vaughan Williams's various musical activities—from choir master, editor, and folk-song collector to composer and conductor—greatly enhanced British musical life; but they also contributed to a mistaken view that his original composition was in some way parochial, designed for domestic consumption. He believed in the value of music education, and wrote pieces for amateurs and service music for the church; but he also displayed great sensitivity to the twentieth-century human condition, projecting a message of peace and reconciliation in works such as *Dona Nobis Pacem* (1936). Moreover, he wrote works of great artistic integrity and imagination that have stood the test of time, not least for choirs, and for all levels of music making.

Vaughan Williams was inspired by great literature and by a lifelong belief that the voice 'can be made the medium of the best and deepest human emotion' (*Vaughan Williams on Music*, ed. D. Manning, Oxford, 2007). Made up of two volumes and organized into sacred and secular works, the current collection is designed to introduce new generations of choral conductors and choirs to Vaughan Williams, sharing his music's variety and timeless quality. There is a mix of familiar and unfamiliar titles. A second aim was to make the pieces, where necessary, match today's scoring and performance needs, improving accessibility and extending their usefulness in a way that would have appealed to Vaughan Williams. At one extreme the arrangements have new piano parts for unaccompanied sections, for example, to lend support, or contain small judicious cuts. Others are arranged in a friendlier key (taking into account the range, also), or for SATB choir from a unison or treble-voice original—the subject matter and content lending itself equally well to adults. At the other end, pieces were selected for their ongoing appeal and suitability, requiring no more than light editorial amendments. In all cases, the harmony, words, and dynamics are unaltered, and my aim has been to respect the integrity and spirit of the original work.

The following commentary, on individual pieces, specifies the changes, sources, and possible uses in performance.

Finally, I wish to record my thanks to Oxford University Press for assisting my research and allowing access to its extensive catalogue, and to The Vaughan Williams Charitable Trust for its kind support.

John Leavitt
2019

Notes on the pieces

Spring from Three Children's Songs
Source: '1. The Singers', OUP, 1930
Suggested programming: Spring concert

This piece, originally written for unison chorus and piano, has been arranged for mixed choir. The piano pedal should be used modestly and according to the harmonic changes in the piece.

The Singers from Three Children's Songs
Source: '2. The Singers', OUP, 1930, renewed in the USA, 1958
Suggested programming: Spring concerts

This piece, originally written for unison chorus and piano, has been arranged for mixed choir. This rhythmic piece requires energetic diction, especially in the softer sections. The piano should be played mostly secco but pedal may be used in places such as bars 17 to 23.

An Invitation from Three Children's Songs
Source: '3. An Invitation', OUP, 1930
Suggested programming: Spring concerts

This piece, originally written for unison chorus and piano, has been arranged for mixed choir. The piano should play mostly secco but pedal may be used in sections such as bars 10 and 12.

Whether men do laugh or weep
Source: 'Whether Men Do Laugh or Weep', OUP, 1931
Suggested programming: Festival or general concert

Changes have been made to the piano layout to facilitate better efficiency between the hands. The piano pedal should be used modestly so as not to blur the musical lines, and should not be used at all in the section with a staccato left hand bass.

John Dory
Source: 'John Dory', OUP, 1934
Suggested programming: General concerts or encores

Changes have been made to the piano layout to facilitate better efficiency between the hands. The piano part is for rehearsal only.

Nothing is here for tears
Source: 'Nothing is here for tears' for SA chorus and piano, OUP, 1936
Suggested programming: Funeral, commemoration, or patriotic concert

This piece has been arranged for SATB voices and piano. The unison vocal parts between bars 4 and 30 have been divided between the contrasting sections of the choir (Sopranos/Tenors and Altos/Basses), and arranged for four-part singing in bars 33–40. Changes have been made to the piano layout for efficiency, and the piano pedal should be used sparingly to avoid blurring the musical lines.

She's like the swallow
Source: 'She's Like the Swallow', Oxford Choral Songs (unison and piano), OUP, 1934
Suggested programming: General concerts

This folksong was originally arranged for unison voices with piano accompaniment. Here, it is rearranged for unaccompanied SATB voices with a soloist. The choral parts conform to the harmonic structure of the original piano part.

Greensleeves
Sources: 'Greensleeves', Vaughan Williams Collected Songs, Vol. 1, OUP, 1934; 'Greensleeves', Oxford Choral Songs (SA and piano), OUP, 1954; 'Greensleeves' for SATB a cappella, OUP, 1945
Suggested programming: Spring or Autumn concerts

An accompanied SATB arrangement of this piece has been created from three sources by Vaughan Williams: a version for solo voice and piano, a version for SA and piano, and an a cappella version for SATB voices. The harmony of the SATB chorals conforms to the original harmonic structure of the piano parts taken from the two accompanied editions. The piano pedal may be used modestly.

Silence and Music
Source: 'Silence and Music', OUP, 1953, renewed in the USA, 1955
Suggested programming: General concert

This piece originates from a cycle of songs for mixed voices entitled, 'A Garland for the Queen': a collection of pieces by ten British composers to mark the occasion of the Coronation of H.M. Queen Elizabeth II. Changes have been made to the piano layout to facilitate better efficiency between the hands. The piano part is for rehearsal only.

Land of our birth

Sources: 'Land of Our Birth' for unison and piano, OUP, 1945; 'A Song of Thanksgiving', OUP, 1945

Suggested programming: Festival or patriotic concert

This arrangement for SATB chorus and piano has been created from two sources: a version for unison voices and piano, and 'A Song of Thanksgiving'. The first three verses draw from the unison version. Verse four then segues into the SATB setting from 'A Song of Thanksgiving' before returning to the unison anthem for the final verse. In this verse, this arrangement mirrors the choral parts from 'A Song of Thanksgiving' to conform with the unison anthem piano part. The vocal parts in bars 54–7 draw upon both settings of the piece. The piano pedal may be used modestly throughout.

Spring

from 'Three Children's Songs'

Frances M. Farrer
(1895–1977)

RALPH VAUGHAN WILLIAMS (1872–1958)
arr. John Leavitt

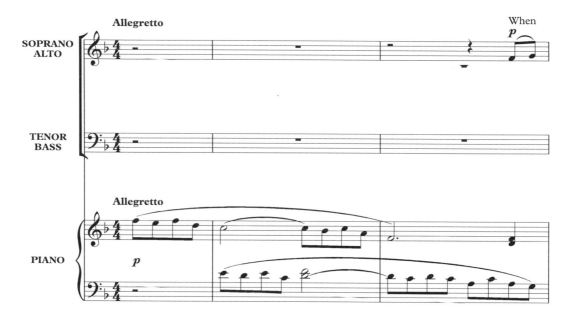

Duration: *c*.2 mins

The Singers
from '*Three Children's Songs*'

Frances M. Farrer
(1895–1977)

RALPH VAUGHAN WILLIAMS (1872–1958)
arr. John Leavitt

Duration: *c.*2 min

S./A. unis.

But what shall we be?

O, we will sing high

T./B. unis.

and

And no-thing on earth shall pre-vent us, A

we will sing low,

fig for your in-dus-try, off you may go, 'Tis sing - - -

Ped.

- ing, 'tis sing - - - ing, 'tis

sing - ing a - lone shall con - tent___ us.

Sam will drive a bus,

Sue will be a dress-mak- er,

sing - - ing, 'tis sing - - ing, 'tis

sing - ing a - lone shall con - tent___ us.

E - li - za - beth, Tom, Har - ri - et, John and Sam and Sue,

Though you have a trade in store O, won't you sing too?

we will sing high and we will sing low, And no-thing on earth shall pre-

-vent us, A fig for your in-dus-try, off you may go, 'Tis

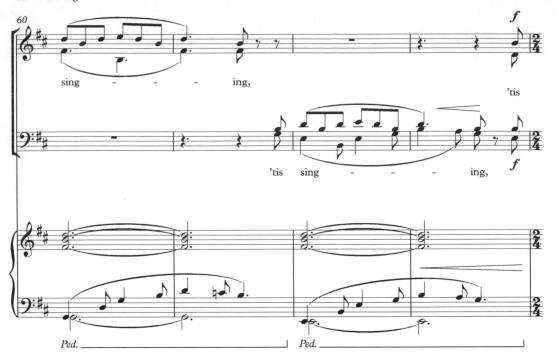

sing - - - ing,   'tis

'tis sing - - - ing,

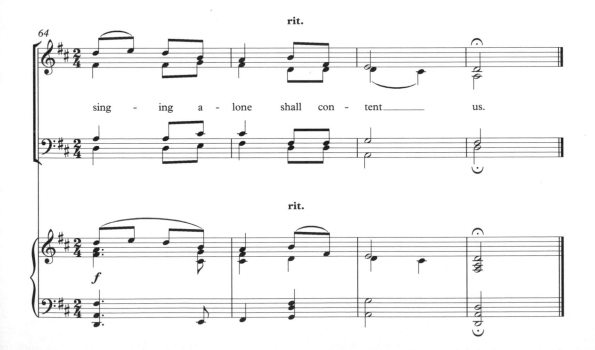

sing - ing a - lone   shall con - tent_____ us.

An Invitation
from 'Three Children's Songs'

Frances M. Farrer
(1895–1977)

RALPH VAUGHAN WILLIAMS (1872–1958)
arr. John Leavitt

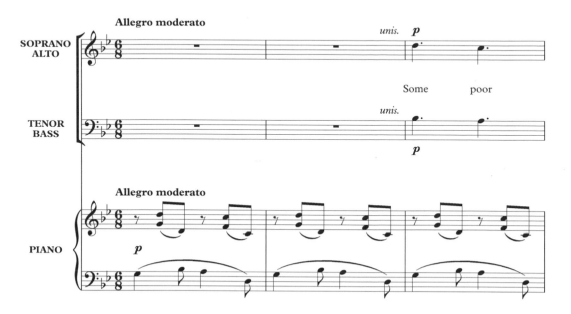

Duration: *c.*3 mins

grass turns brown, And there's ne - ver a morn - ing black-bird to sing

Out - side their win-dow to tell them of Spring.

Pi - ty poor fel - lows who live in the town, Where the

gri - my smuts come tum - bling down; Here in the coun - try the

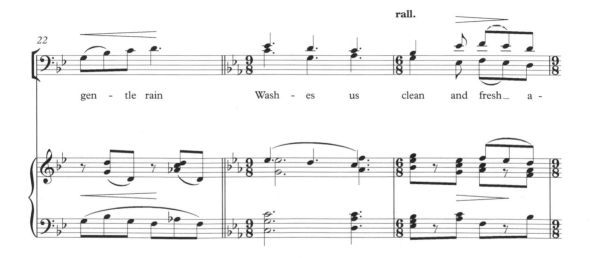

gen - tle rain Wash - es us clean and fresh a -

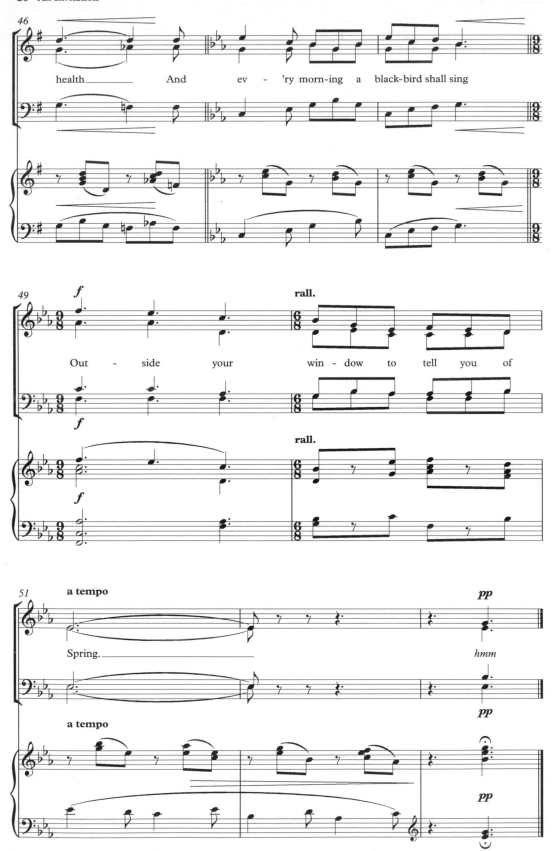

health _____ And ev - 'ry morn-ing a black-bird shall sing

Out - side your win - dow to tell you of

Spring. _____ hmm

Whether men do laugh or weep

Words from
Campion and Rosseter's *Book of Airs* (1601)

RALPH VAUGHAN WILLIAMS (1872–1958)
ed. John Leavitt

Duration: *c*.3 mins

There is un-der-neath the sun   no-thing in true   earn –   –   –   –   est

* First sopranos may join second sopranos for the bracketed passage, in which case altos sing the small notes.

and the world___ is but___ a

and the world___ is but___ a

and the world___ is but___ a

and the world___ is but___ a

play.___

play.___

play.___

play.___

John Dory

English folksong
arr. RALPH VAUGHAN WILLIAMS (1872–1958)
ed. John Leavitt

Duration: c.3 mins

19

John of France, King John___

John of France, King John___

France - a; John Do - ry could well of his cour - te - sie, But
me - a, And all the churls in mer - ry Eng - land, I'll

France - a; John Do - ry could well of his cour - te - sie, But
me - a, And all the churls in mer - ry Eng - land, I'll

22

p

___ of France, King John of

p

___ of France, King John of

p

fell down in a trance - a, but fell down in a
bring them bound to thee - a, I'll bring them bound to

p

fell down in a trance - a, but fell down in a
bring them bound to thee - a, I'll bring them bound to

p

36

good black bark, With fif-ty good oars on a side.   6. They
to his lot,__ What - ev - er should be - tide.____

side - a, with fif-ty good oars on a side.____ 6. They
-tide - a, what - ev - er should be - tide.____ 7. The

__ with fif-ty good oars on a side.____
__ what - ev - er should be - tide. Dub - a-dub

side, with__ fif-ty good oars on a side.____ 6. They
-tide, what - ev - er should be - tide.____ 7. The

39

Dub - a-dub dub, dub - a-dub dub, dub - a-dub dub,

dub, dub - a-dub dub, dub - a-dub dub, dub - a-dub

roar - ing can - non then were plied, And dub - a-dub went the
(8.) grap - pling hooks were brought at length, The brown bill and the

roar - ing can - non then were plied, And dub - a-dub went the
(8.) grap - pling hooks were brought at length, The brown bill and the

Nothing is here for tears

John Milton (adap.)
(1608–74)

RALPH VAUGHAN WILLIAMS (1872–1958)
arr. John Leavitt

No-thing is here for tears,

No-thing to wail; No-thing but well and fair, And what may

Duration: *c.*2 mins

She's like the swallow

Newfoundland folksong
arr. RALPH VAUGHAN WILLIAMS (1872–1958)
arr. for SATB choir by John Leavitt

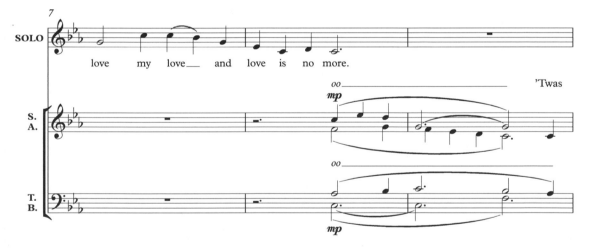

Duration: *c*.2 mins

This song is taken from *Folk Songs from Newfoundland*, collected and edited by Maud Karpeles.

Greensleeves

English folksong
arr. RALPH VAUGHAN WILLIAMS (1872–1958)
arr. for SATB choir by John Leavitt

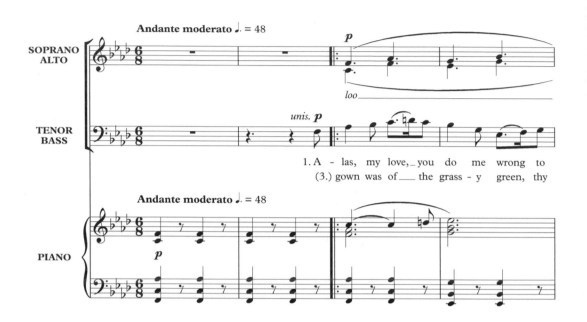

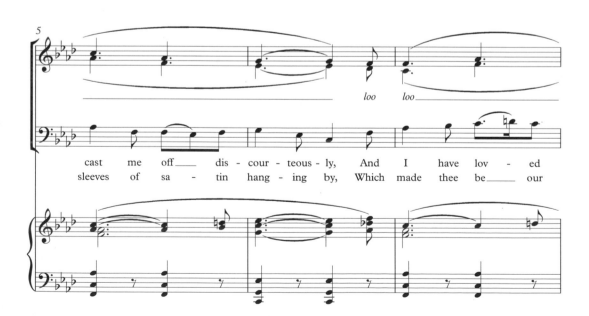

Duration: *c.*3 mins

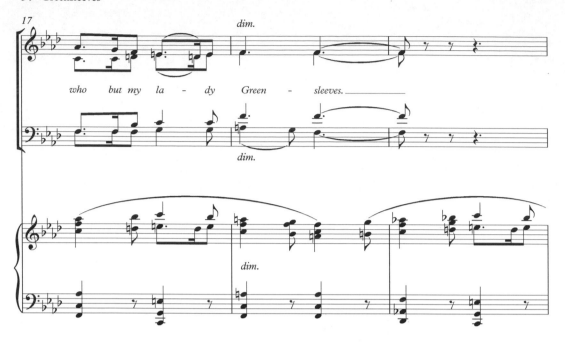

who but my la - dy Green - sleeves.

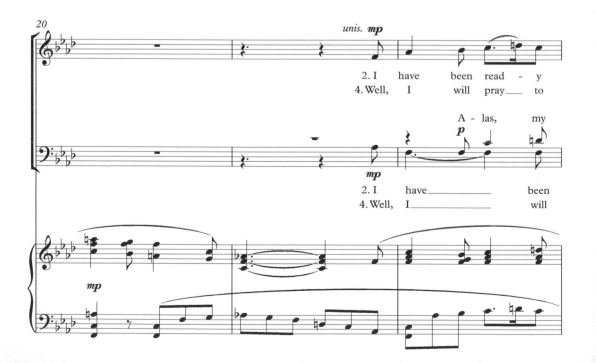

2. I   have   been   read - y
4. Well,   I   will   pray___   to

A - las,   my

2. I   have_____   been
4. Well,   I_____   will

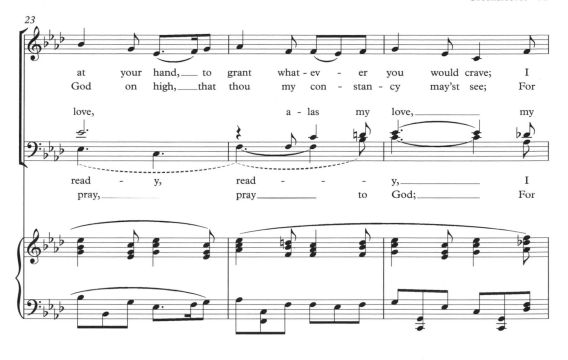

at   your hand,___ to grant   what - ev - er   you   would crave;   I
God   on   high,___that thou   my con - stan - cy   may'st see;   For

love,   a - las my love,_____   my

read - y,   read - - y,_____   I
pray,___   pray_____ to God;___   For

have   both wa - ged   life   and land,___ your   love___and good - will
I   am still___ thy   lov - er   true;   come once___ a - gain___and

love,_____   you do   me   wrong,_____   you do   me

have_____   wa - ged   life   your good - will
I'm_____   thy   lov - er;   come a - gain   and

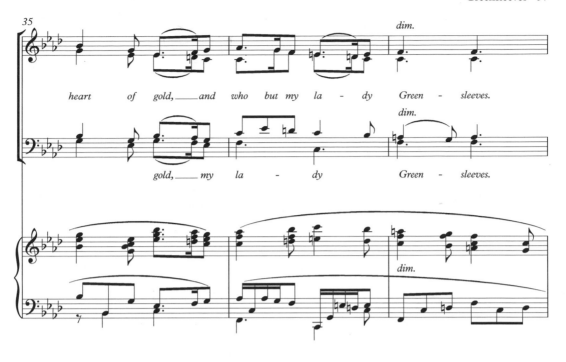

heart of gold, ___ and who but my la - dy Green - sleeves.

gold, ___ my la - dy Green - sleeves.

1.

2. rit.

p

loo ___ loo ___ loo loo ___

unis. p

3. Thy loo loo loo loo ___

to the memory of
Charles Villiers Stanford, and his Blue Bird

Silence and Music

Ursula Wood
(1911–2007)

RALPH VAUGHAN WILLIAMS (1872–1958)
ed. John Leavitt

Duration: *c*.4 mins

Land of our birth

from 'A Song of Thanksgiving'

Rudyard Kipling
(1865–1936)

RALPH VAUGHAN WILLIAMS (1872–1958)
arr. for SATB choir by John Leavitt

Duration: *c.*5 mins

2. Fa - ther in Heav'n who lov - est all,   O help thy

chil - dren when they   call,   That they may   build from age to

age   An un - de - fil - ed he - ri - tage.

thee,   Head,   heart and hand through the years

to   be.